# HOW TO BE AN ASTRONAUT
## AND OTHER SPACE JOBS

nosy crow

D1335829

To budding space cadets, the sky isn't the limit, it's the start! Be kind to each other; the universe is a big place but so far we're the only humans we've got, so enjoy your life, and help others enjoy theirs (thanks Simon N Ricketts)! S.K

To all the the people that dreamed about being an astronaut when they were kids . . . S.L

First published 2019 by Nosy Crow Ltd
The Crow's Nest, 14 Baden Place
Crosby Row, London SE1 1YW
www.nosycrow.com

ISBN 978 1 78800 521 0 (HB)
ISBN 978 1 78800 444 2 (PB)

Nosy Crow and associated logos are trademarks
and/or registered trademarks of Nosy Crow Ltd

Text © Dr Sheila Kanani 2019
Illustrations © Sol Linero 2019

The right of Dr Sheila Kanani to be identified as the author and Sol Linero
to be identified as the illustrator of this work has been asserted.

A CIP catalogue record for this book is available from the British Library.

Printed in Italy

Papers used by Nosy Crow are made from wood grown in
sustainable forests.

10 9 8 7 6 5 4 3 2 1 (HB)
10 9 8 7 6 5 4 3 2 1 (PB)

# WHAT IS SPACE?

Space is massive! Space is bigger than anyone can imagine! Space goes on further than the eye can see! But what actually is it?

Space starts **100 kilometres above Earth** – that's **ten times** the height that **most aeroplanes fly at.** It is very dark and quiet up there, with no air to breathe. But that doesn't mean it is empty. There are **loads of cool things in space,** like planets and stars, comets and asteroids, gas and dust.

SUN

MERCURY    VENUS    EARTH    MARS

Stars are enormous balls of burning-hot gas. **The Sun is a star.** Because it is so hot it gives off energy, which almost all living things on Earth need to live. Plants use energy from the Sun to grow, and animals (including humans) need these plants to eat, and the warmth and light from the Sun to survive.

### DID YOU KNOW?
There are more stars in space than there are grains of sand on the whole Earth!

4

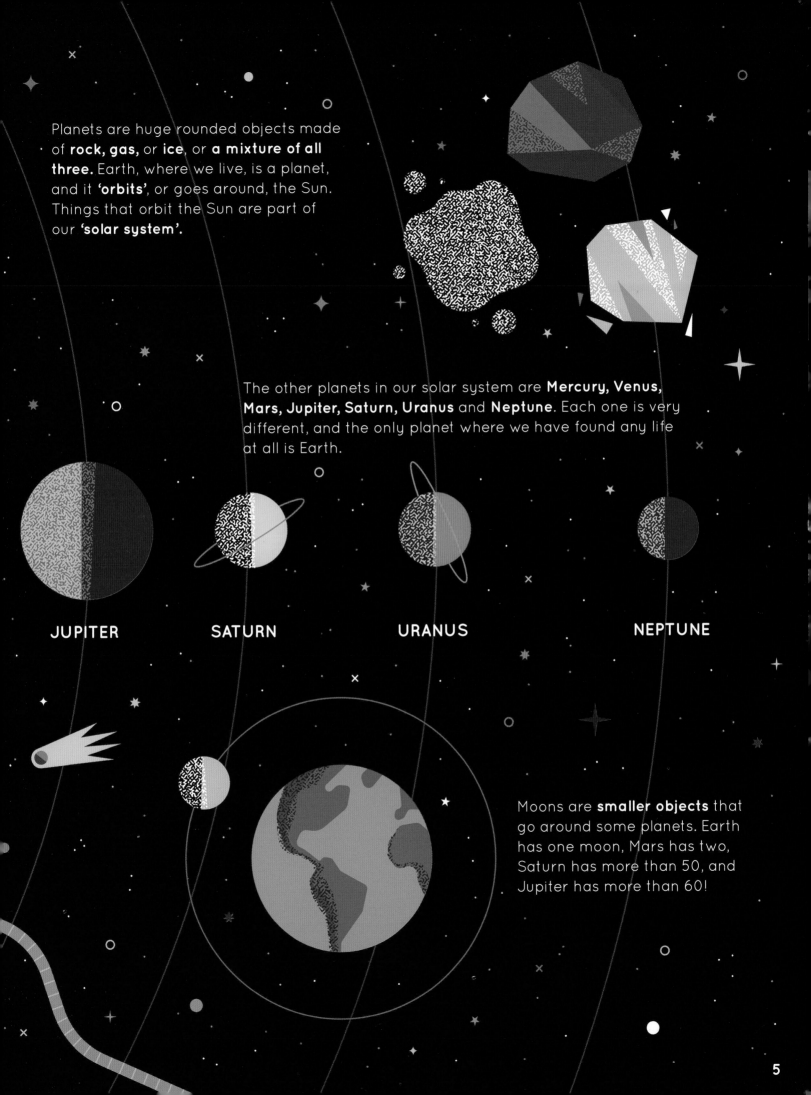

Planets are huge rounded objects made of **rock, gas,** or **ice,** or **a mixture of all three.** Earth, where we live, is a planet, and it **'orbits'**, or goes around, the Sun. Things that orbit the Sun are part of our **'solar system'.**

The other planets in our solar system are **Mercury, Venus, Mars, Jupiter, Saturn, Uranus** and **Neptune**. Each one is very different, and the only planet where we have found any life at all is Earth.

**JUPITER**

**SATURN**

**URANUS**

**NEPTUNE**

Moons are **smaller objects** that go around some planets. Earth has one moon, Mars has two, Saturn has more than 50, and Jupiter has more than 60!

# WHY EXPLORE SPACE ?

Space explorers are looking for all kinds of things, from new planets to alien life!

We now know that there are **other solar systems in space**, where other stars have got other planets orbiting around them. Planets in other solar systems are called **'exoplanets'**. We've found **almost 4,000 exoplanets** so far, but there are many still to discover. If we are lucky, we might even find a new planet that could be enough like Earth for us to live on.

Some space scientists are **looking for aliens!** We haven't found them yet, but that doesn't mean they don't exist. Maybe space is too big for us to find them. Perhaps they are very good at hiding, or maybe they communicate in a different way, so we can't hear them?

We come in peace!

?

Out of all the planets we have ever found, Earth is the only one with life on it, so by exploring space we can see just how special our planet is and think about how we should **look after our world.**

One of the **most important** reasons to explore space is to make us think more carefully about life on our own planet, and what Earth might be like in the future.

In order to explore space, we need people who work in the 'space industry'. Jobs vary from . . .

And, of course . . . astronauts!

engineers

and scientists,

to doctors

and chefs.

# THE HISTORY OF
# SPACE EXPLORATION

For thousands of years, humans have been fascinated by the question of what is 'up there'. This is because no matter where you are in the world, you can see the Sun, Moon and some planets and stars, just with your eyes.

Aglaonike was the first known female astronomer in ancient Greece. She could predict lunar eclipses and was sometimes called a witch!

The first telescope was made by the German-Dutch astronomer Hans Lippershey.

**200 - 100 BC**

**753 BC - 476 AD**

**499 AD**

**1608**

**1609- 1630**

The ancient Romans named seven bright objects in the sky: Mercury, Venus, Mars, Jupiter, Saturn, as well as the Sun and Moon, which they called Apollo and Diana!

Other astronomers, such as Galileo, started using more and more powerful telescopes to discover planets, moons and stars.

The Indian mathematician and astronomer Aryabhata came up with the idea of the force of gravity to explain why objects do not fall off the Earth.

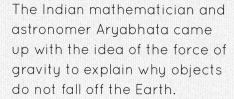

**DID YOU KNOW?**
Russian astronauts are sometimes called 'cosmonauts'.

A Russian astronaut called Yuri Gagarin orbited Earth once. He had to use a parachute to land. A few weeks later, the Americans sent Alan Shepard into space.

The Russian *Sputnik 1* satellite became the first ever human-made object to orbit the Earth!
This started the Space Race – a battle between the Russians and the Americans to land on the moon first.

A dog named Laika was sent by the Russians into space inside the *Sputnik 2* satellite.

A Russian astronaut called Valentina Tereshkova became the first woman in space.

| 1940-1949 | 1957 | 1959 | 1961 | 1963 | 1969 |

In the 1940s, humans started launching rockets further and further into space.

The Russians landed a satellite called *Luna 2* on the Moon.

America won the Space Race when they sent Neil Armstrong, Buzz Aldrin and Michael Collins to the moon on the *Apollo 11* spacecraft.

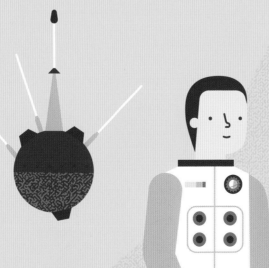

9

# EXPLORING
# SPACE TODAY

Today, we use space technology in ways we couldn't have imagined 50 years ago.

**The future** of space exploration is **full of opportunities** for the next generation of scientists and engineers. There are plans to visit moons of Saturn and Jupiter, head to Uranus, launch telescopes to delve deep into space, search for aliens, learn more about asteroids and to get closer to the Sun than ever before. Space agencies across the Earth also want to take humans back to the Moon, and **eventually land humans on Mars.**

**Satellites** do lots of **different jobs. Some look back on the Earth** and measure weather, changes in the climate, and the number of people living in a particular place. **Others travel to the edges of the solar system** to look at distant objects like Pluto and Ceres.

### DID YOU KNOW?
In the near future, 'normal people' might be able to travel into space for a holiday!

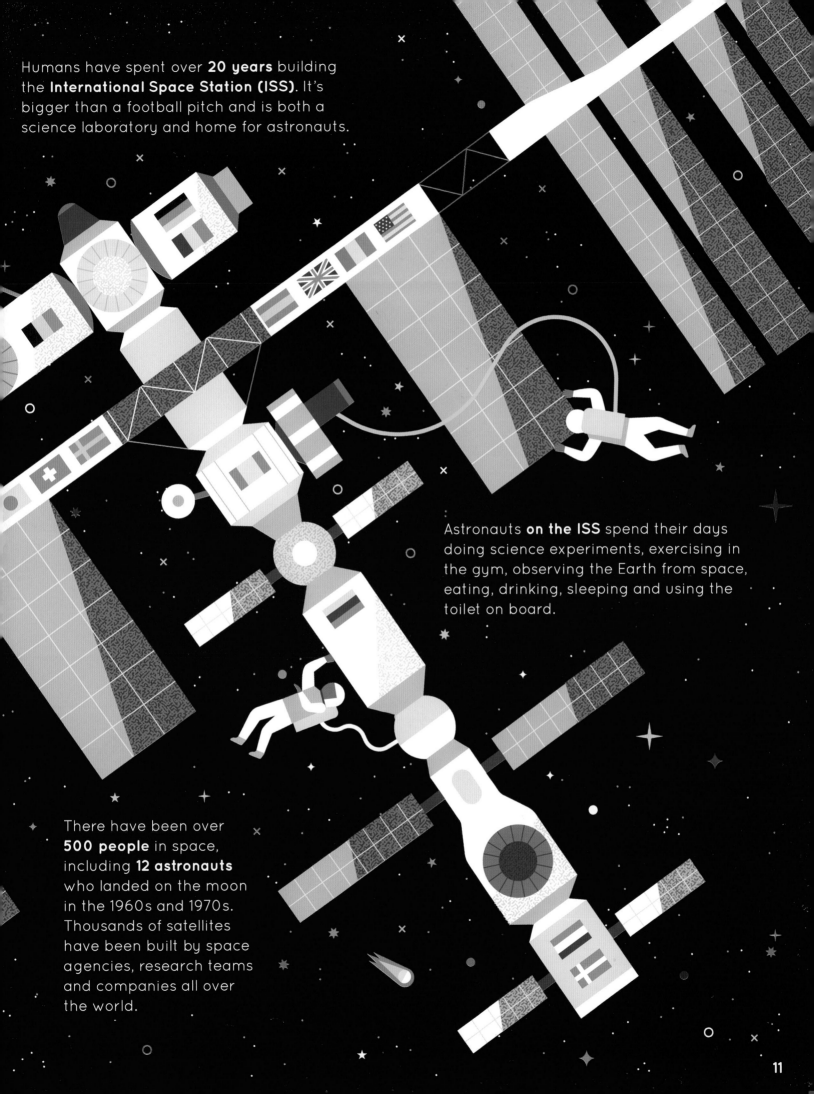

Humans have spent over **20 years** building the **International Space Station (ISS)**. It's bigger than a football pitch and is both a science laboratory and home for astronauts.

Astronauts **on the ISS** spend their days doing science experiments, exercising in the gym, observing the Earth from space, eating, drinking, sleeping and using the toilet on board.

There have been over **500 people** in space, including **12 astronauts** who landed on the moon in the 1960s and 1970s. Thousands of satellites have been built by space agencies, research teams and companies all over the world.

# HOW DO YOU BECOME AN ASTRONAUT?

First of all, you must **work in science, engineering or the military** for at least three years. Being a pilot helps, but it isn't essential, as astronauts now take on different roles in the spacecraft. One might be **a pilot,** another **a scientist,** and another could be **a doctor.**

**Languages** are important – most astronauts have to be able to speak **English** and **Russian** to communicate with other astronauts in their team.

Some space agencies also say you **must be a certain height.** Usually you have to be between 157 cm and 190.5 cm tall – any taller and you won't be **able to fit inside the spacecraft!**

190.5 cm

157cm

If you want to become an astronaut scientist, you should do a **university degree** after school. There are hundreds of **science subjects** to choose, from physics to medicine.

Having **other hobbies** is important as well. Astronauts enjoy lots of different activities, from reading and playing the guitar . . .

to hiking and long-distance running.

So, if you are **interested in science, enjoy sports** and other hobbies and think you could **work well in a team**, then you could be an astronaut! But there's a lot of training to do first . . .

# WHAT KIND OF
# TRAINING
## DO ASTRONAUTS HAVE TO DO?

**Basic training is a bit like going to school.** You **learn everything** from the history of spaceflight and electrical engineering, to Russian language and first aid.

You also learn all about the ISS, from **navigation and control** to **life support systems** and **robotics.**

$$\frac{x-ab}{\sqrt{a+b}}$$

Your mind is also tested. Astronauts are expected to have **good memory, concentration** and **problem-solving skills.** You should be able to **understand other people's feelings** and not get angry or too homesick.

Astronauts have to be **fit and healthy.** To test their bodies, they do **unusual exercises** like sitting in a **centrifuge.** You sit inside a small pod and a metal arm spins you around, which can make you feel very sick. This tests how a person might feel in a rocket during take-off and landing.

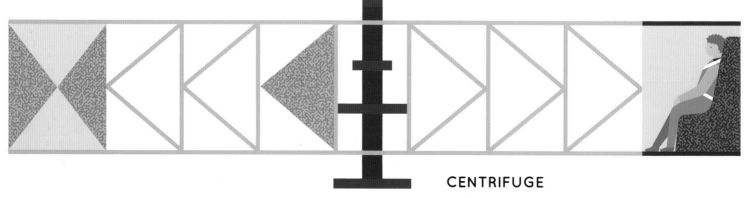

CENTRIFUGE

Astronauts also have to get used to **'microgravity'.** Gravity is the force that attracts you to the Earth and stops you floating away. In space, there is **very little gravity**, which feels strange.

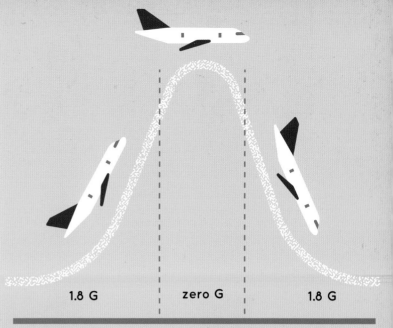

1.8 G     zero G     1.8 G

**Astronauts practise** by going on a special plane (known as the **'vomit comet'**), which flies up and down **like a rollercoaster** and makes you feel like you're floating.

**Finally, astronauts are given a mission to train for.** They go through every experiment they will do up in space and get to know the other two astronauts in their team. They also **learn what to do in an emergency** (including how to fix the space toilet!).

### DID YOU KNOW?
Swimming deep underwater feels a bit like space, so astronauts learn how to scuba dive in a giant swimming pool with parts of the ISS.

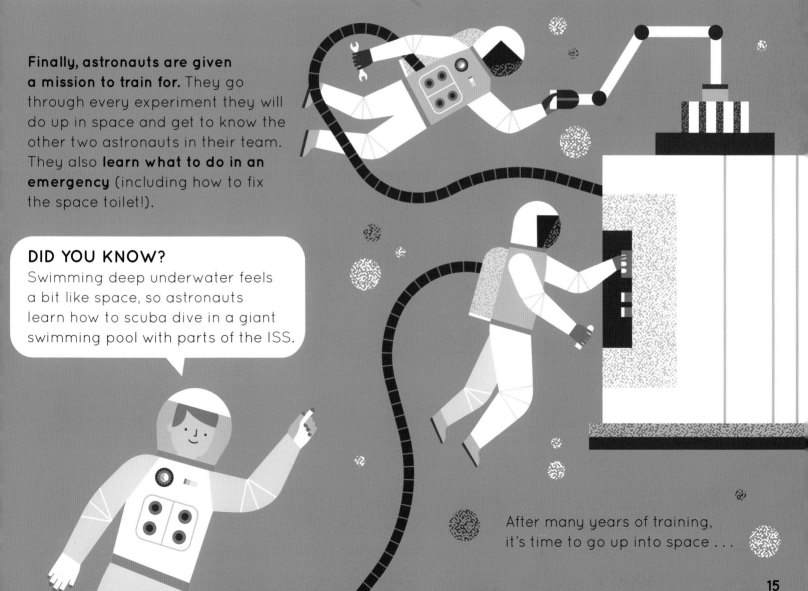

After many years of training, it's time to go up into space . . .

# WHAT DOES IT FEEL LIKE TO GO INTO SPACE?

**The Soyuz capsule** takes astronauts to and from space. It is about the **size of a van** and sits on top of a huge rocket. Astronauts crawl into the capsule through a hatch and sit in a seat made specially for them.

**During launch,** it feels like gravity is getting stronger because the rocket is moving so quickly. This is called **'G force'.** It feels a bit like **riding a rollercoaster, surfing a giant wave** or, as the Canadian astronaut Chris Hadfield put it, **"like a gorilla was squishing you and then threw you off a cliff"**!

**After five minutes,** the rocket detaches from the capsule and, **four minutes later,** the astronauts in the capsule feel **weightless.**

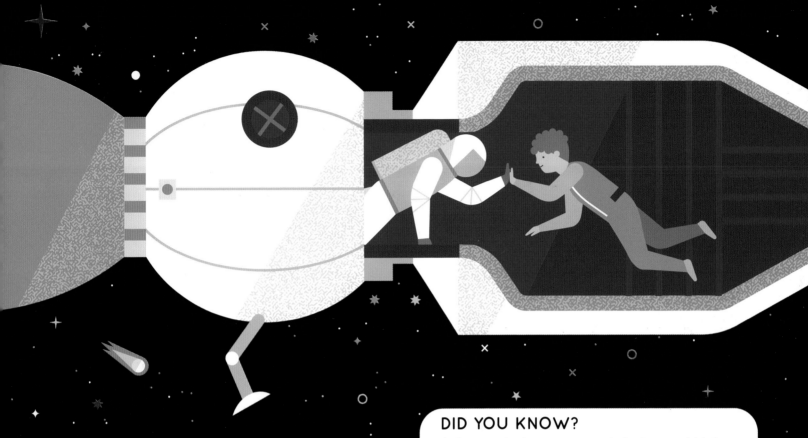

Once the capsule reaches the **International Space Station,** it has to be **docked** or parked on the space station. Then the astronauts climb aboard the ISS and meet the other three astronauts already on board.

The ISS orbits the Earth **faster than the speed of sound,** but the astronauts on board **don't feel like they are moving.** Instead, they feel microgravity, which makes them **float about like a superhero.**

Sometimes astronauts have to get out of the ISS while it is orbiting the Earth. This is called **a spacewalk,** and might be for a science experiment outside the spacecraft or to fix something.

Wearing a spacesuit, they exit the spacecraft through a **special door called an airlock** and then tie themselves and their tools to the main spacecraft using a cord called a **'tether'** so they don't float away.

**DID YOU KNOW?**
Astronauts have a special piece of Velcro inside their helmets, so they can scratch their noses.

Velcro

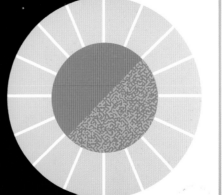

# WHAT DO ASTRONAUTS ACTUALLY DO
# ON THE SPACE STATION?

Astronauts carry out experiments in space. They try to grow plants, watch how animals react in space and test their own bodies.

Astronauts eat dried or packet food and tortilla wraps instead of bread to avoid crumbs, which float around and damage equipment.

ISS PRESSO

Sauces like ketchup are allowed, but no salt or pepper or the grains would float away.

There are no fridges, but there is an oven to make hot food.

Astronauts **can't have showers** as water turns into floating droplets. Instead, they **use wet wipes** and clean their hair using **dry shampoo**.

To **brush their teeth,** they suck water into their mouths from a pouch and swallow the toothpaste.

A **space toilet** is like a vacuum cleaner: you aim into the hole and the waste is sucked down a tube. Wee is recycled into drinking water, while **poo is frozen and thrown away.** It burns up in the Earth's atmosphere and can be mistaken for a shooting star!

Astronauts have to **exercise for two hours every day** because the microgravity weakens their bodies.

Astronauts **sleep** in sleeping bags attached to the walls so they don't float away. Eye masks block out the light.

# WHAT IS IT LIKE ON
# THE MOON?

Only 12 astronauts have ever been on the Moon and they've all been men. Hopefully this will change in the future as more people have the chance to go into space.

To walk on the Moon, astronauts wear **spacesuits with nappies** inside them because they could spend hours there.

**Spacesuits are very bulky,** which makes it **difficult to bend your knees** or see your own feet. As the Moon has lower gravity than Earth, walking becomes quite clumsy, and you end up bouncing along like a bunny rabbit. It also means you can **jump higher** and **kick a ball further** than you could on Earth!

The **US flag** left by Buzz Aldrin and Neil Armstrong in 1969 is **still on the Moon,** and a lot of other stuff has been left over the years, from cameras to golf balls!

Because there is **no weather,** there is **no wind.** This means that footprints made by astronauts in the 1970s **are still there.**

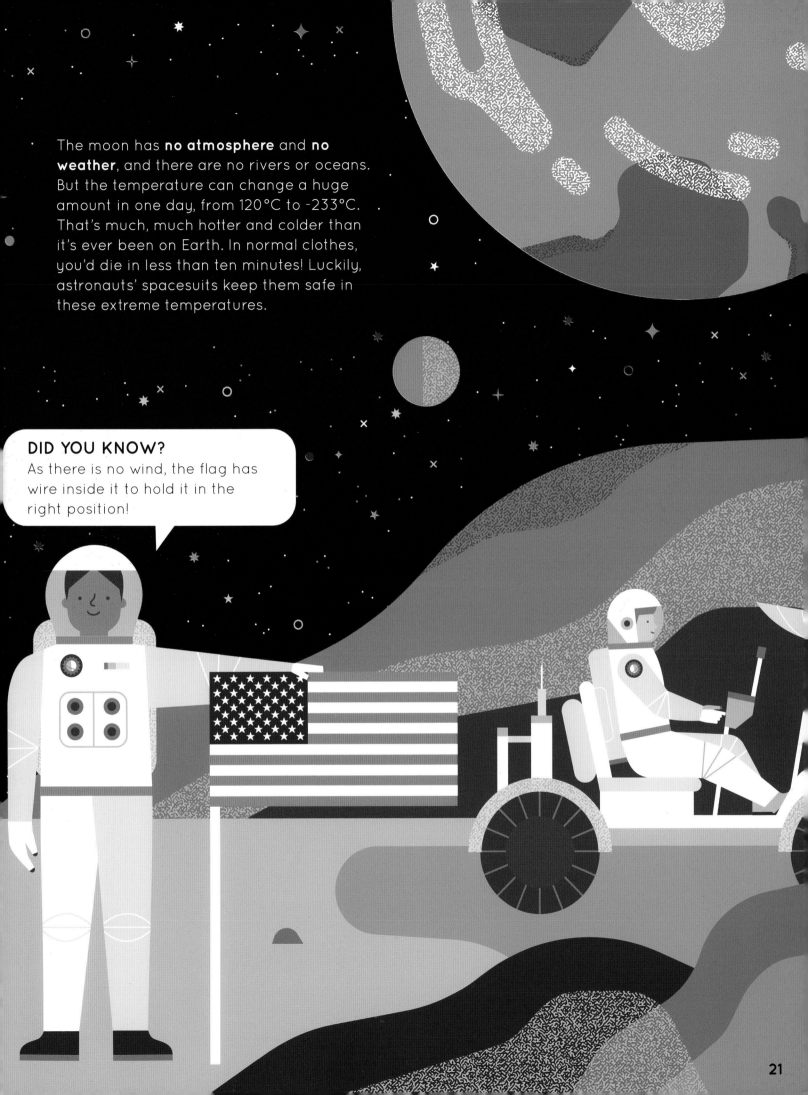

The moon has **no atmosphere** and **no weather**, and there are no rivers or oceans. But the temperature can change a huge amount in one day, from 120°C to -233°C. That's much, much hotter and colder than it's ever been on Earth. In normal clothes, you'd die in less than ten minutes! Luckily, astronauts' spacesuits keep them safe in these extreme temperatures.

**DID YOU KNOW?**
As there is no wind, the flag has wire inside it to hold it in the right position!

# HOW DO ASTRONAUTS GET
# BACK TO EARTH?

**Once the mission is finished,** the astronauts get into their spacesuits, crawl into the **Soyuz capsule,** and **ride back to Earth.**

The Soyuz capsule **doesn't have wings or wheels,** so it does not land back on the Earth like an aeroplane. Instead, when it gets close to the land, **parachutes come out and little rocket engines fire to slow it down.** The landing is bumpy, and the capsule can land on the ground or in the sea. The astronauts on board feel a bit like they're inside a washing machine!

ORBIT

ATMOSPHERE

ENTRY

COMMUNICATION
BLACKOUT

KAZAKHSTAN

LANDING
ZONE

Since the astronauts have been in space for **six months,** floating around in **microgravity,** they suddenly feel very heavy and are unable to stand or walk at first. So, the medical team have to pick them up and put them into chairs. **It can take months for their bodies to get back to normal.**

When astronauts **aren't in space,** they are still working! They do interviews, meet the public and talk to school children.

**DID YOU KNOW?**
While it takes six hours to get to the ISS, it only takes three and a half hours to get home!

They train for **future missions** or support current missions. They might talk to astronauts who are in space, or work in the swimming pool, training other astronauts to do spacewalks.

They also **study the data they've collected** in space or do experiments on Earth. And they must keep fit and healthy so that they can go into space on another mission!

# WHAT OTHER KINDS OF SPACE JOBS ARE THERE?

For every astronaut that goes to the International Space Station, there are hundreds of people working hard to get them there. But what do these people actually do?

**Spacesuit designers** look at each astronaut and mission, then they design spacesuits to **fit that astronaut exactly.** Spacesuits need to keep astronauts comfortable, at the right temperature and with air to breathe.

## DID YOU KNOW?
Spacewalks can last for hours, so spacesuits have to be able to absorb a lot of sweat!

**Computer engineers** create robots that can drive around planets, drill holes, take photos and decode information.

Computer engineers also write the programmes needed to **make the technology work.**

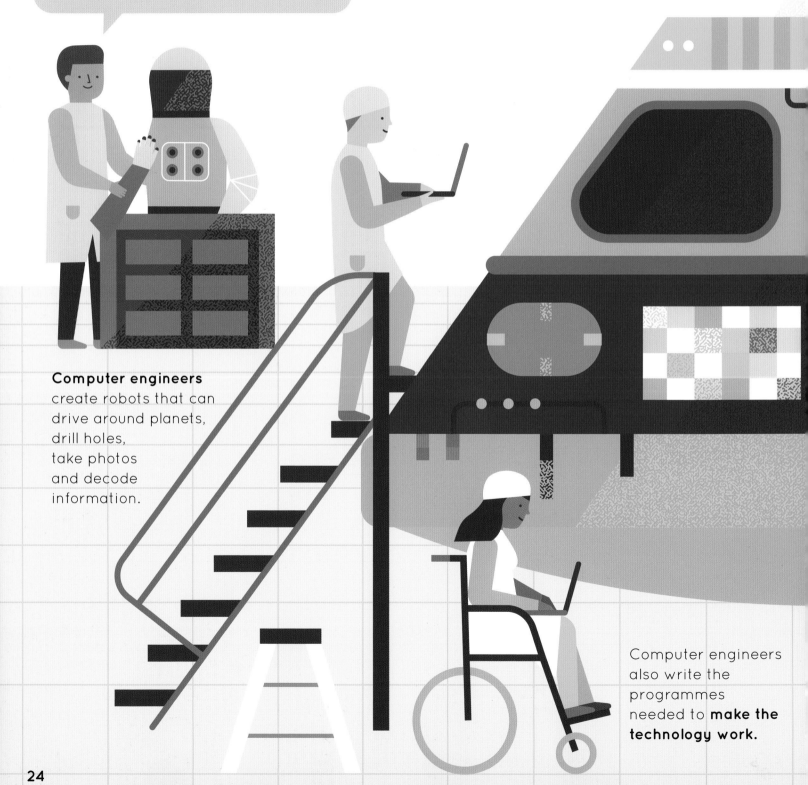

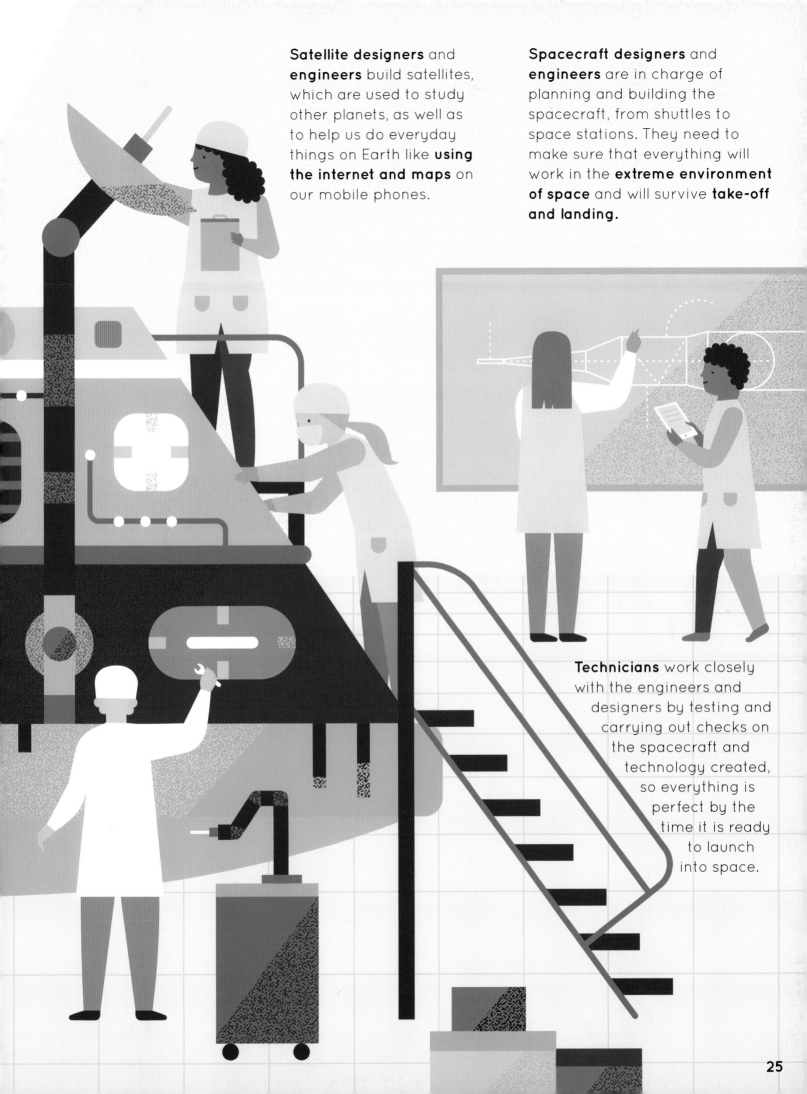

**Satellite designers** and **engineers** build satellites, which are used to study other planets, as well as to help us do everyday things on Earth like **using the internet and maps** on our mobile phones.

**Spacecraft designers** and **engineers** are in charge of planning and building the spacecraft, from shuttles to space stations. They need to make sure that everything will work in the **extreme environment of space** and will survive **take-off and landing.**

**Technicians** work closely with the engineers and designers by testing and carrying out checks on the spacecraft and technology created, so everything is perfect by the time it is ready to launch into space.

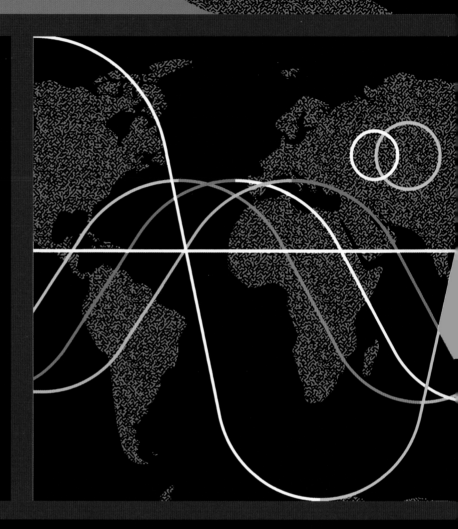

## ARE YOU GOOD AT PROBLEM-SOLVING? THEN A JOB IN

# MISSION CONTROL

## MIGHT BE FOR YOU.

Many experts, from **communicators** to **mathematicians,** work in Mission Control. These people check that the astronauts are safe and well, track where the spacecraft is travelling to and make sure that the rockets launch successfully.

**Flight directors** are in charge of the whole team. They sometimes have to make quick, important decisions to keep the astronauts safe.

FLIGHT DIRECTOR

FLIGHT ACTIVITIES

GROUND CONTROL

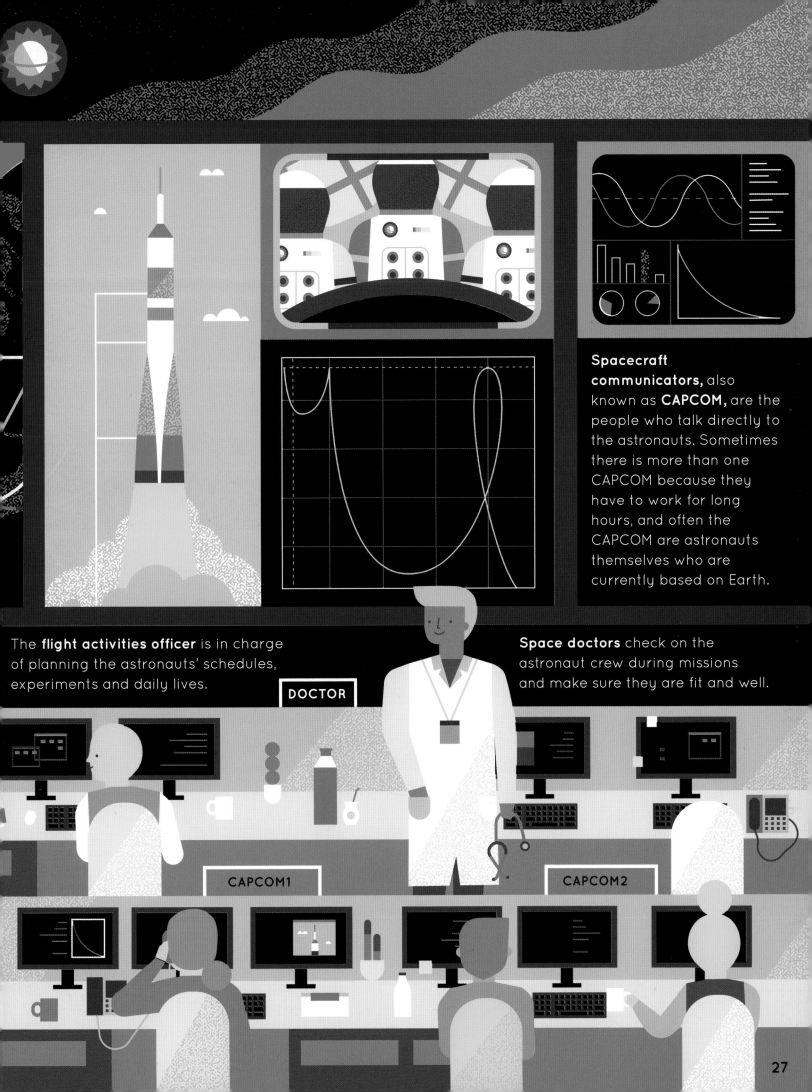

**Spacecraft communicators,** also known as **CAPCOM,** are the people who talk directly to the astronauts. Sometimes there is more than one CAPCOM because they have to work for long hours, and often the CAPCOM are astronauts themselves who are currently based on Earth.

The **flight activities officer** is in charge of planning the astronauts' schedules, experiments and daily lives.

DOCTOR

**Space doctors** check on the astronaut crew during missions and make sure they are fit and well.

CAPCOM1

CAPCOM2

# DO YOU LOVE DOING EXPERIMENTS? THEN BECOME A
# SPACE SCIENTIST.

There are all kinds of science jobs in the space industry, from chemists who grow crystals in space, to psychotherapists who work with the human brain, studying thoughts and feelings.

**Planetary scientists** look at **planets and objects** in the solar system.

They might use spacecraft such as the *Cassini*, which **orbited Saturn for almost 14 years**, taking photographs and studying the planet, then sent the data back to Earth to be investigated.

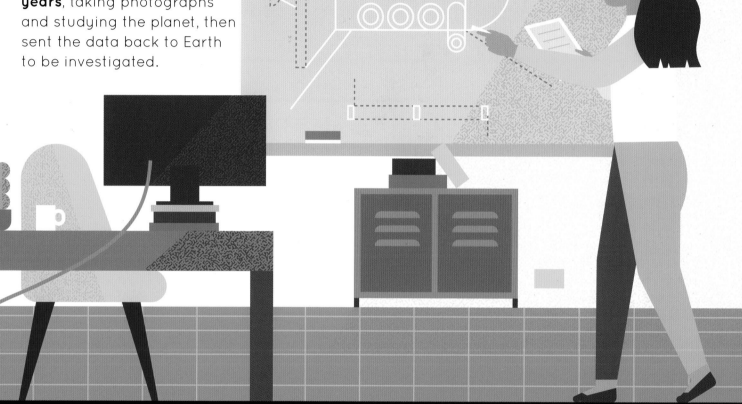

**Exoplanet hunters** look for planets outside our solar system, orbiting stars far away from the Sun. We have found almost 4,000 of these planets already. One day it might even be possible for humans or robots to visit these planets.

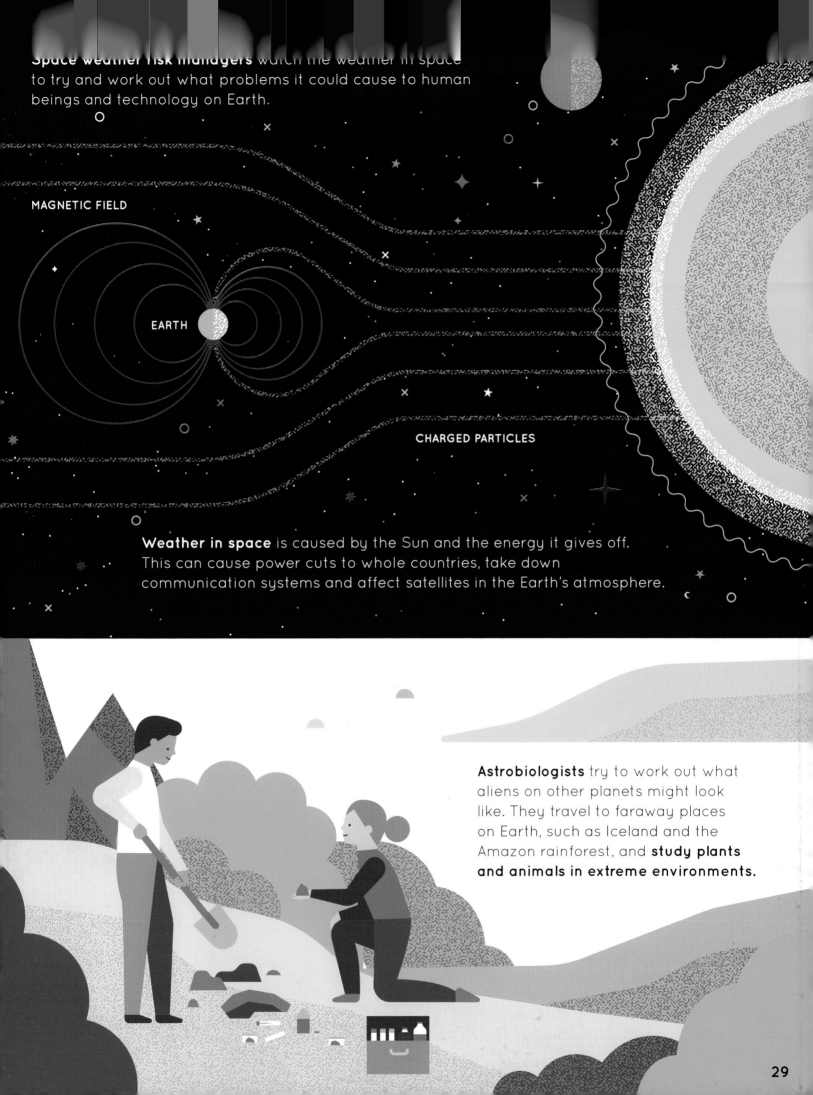

**Space weather risk managers** watch the weather in space to try and work out what problems it could cause to human beings and technology on Earth.

MAGNETIC FIELD

EARTH

CHARGED PARTICLES

**Weather in space** is caused by the Sun and the energy it gives off. This can cause power cuts to whole countries, take down communication systems and affect satellites in the Earth's atmosphere.

**Astrobiologists** try to work out what aliens on other planets might look like. They travel to faraway places on Earth, such as Iceland and the Amazon rainforest, and **study plants and animals in extreme environments.**

# WHAT ABOUT THE MORE
# UNUSUAL SPACE JOBS?

Some specialists work in **space outreach**, organising workshops, activities and talks to teach adults and children more about space.

A **space lawyer** takes care of any legal work. They are often in charge of writing up agreements between different space agencies and answering questions like **"Who owns the minerals on the Moon?"** or **"Whose fault is it if two satellites crash into each other in space?"**

If you enjoy selling, you could be a **spacecraft salesperson.** They show and sell spacecraft to space agencies, and must be persuasive enough to sell it for the best price possible. Or you could be a **space underwriter,** who organises insurance for a satellite. Their job is to make sure that a satellite remains safe from when it launches until the end of its life.

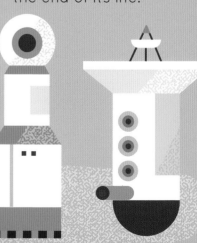

Some space scientists **advise film directors** who are writing films set in space. Without these experts, some films would be incorrect or wouldn't make sense.

Others work as **press officers** or **communication managers**, teaching astronauts how to give good interviews or managing their social media.

If you like food, then maybe you could become a **space chef?** Chefs have to make the meals yummy, but they have to be safe to eat in microgravity (no crumbs, remember!) and the food has to last a long time.

Often meals like scrambled eggs, soups and casseroles are **'dehydrated'** (all the water is taken out of them) so that the rocket is not too heavy. Then, once they reach the ISS, astronauts can rehydrate their meals by adding boiling water.

**DID YOU KNOW?**
Your sense of taste is not as good in space, so food needs to have lots of flavour.

# GET INVOLVED

If you would like to learn more about space jobs or working in the space industry, there are many things you can do . . .

You can join a local astronomy society, become a member of a space organisation, go to space schools and space camps all across the UK or even internationally, or perhaps you might want to set up your own astronomy group! To begin with, all you need is a passion and a curiosity, and hopefully clear skies!

## USEFUL ORGANISATIONS AND WEBSITES INCLUDE:

The Royal Astronomical Society www.ras.ac.uk
European Space Education Resource Office www.stem.org.uk/esero
Space Careers UK www.spacecareers.uk
Space School UK www.spaceschool.co.uk
Space Careers quiz www.destinationspace.uk/meet-space-crew/find-your-role-space-crew
ESA (European Space Agency) www.esa.int/esaKIDSen
NASA (National Aeronautics and Space Administration) www.nasa.gov/kidsclub/index.html

Amateur astronomy organisations:
The Federation of Astronomical Societies www.fedastro.org.uk/fas
British Astronomical Association www.britastro.org
Society for Popular Astronomy www.popastro.com/main_spa1/youngstargazers

In the future, we might be able to go on holiday to the Moon. Use your stickers to imagine what it might look like!

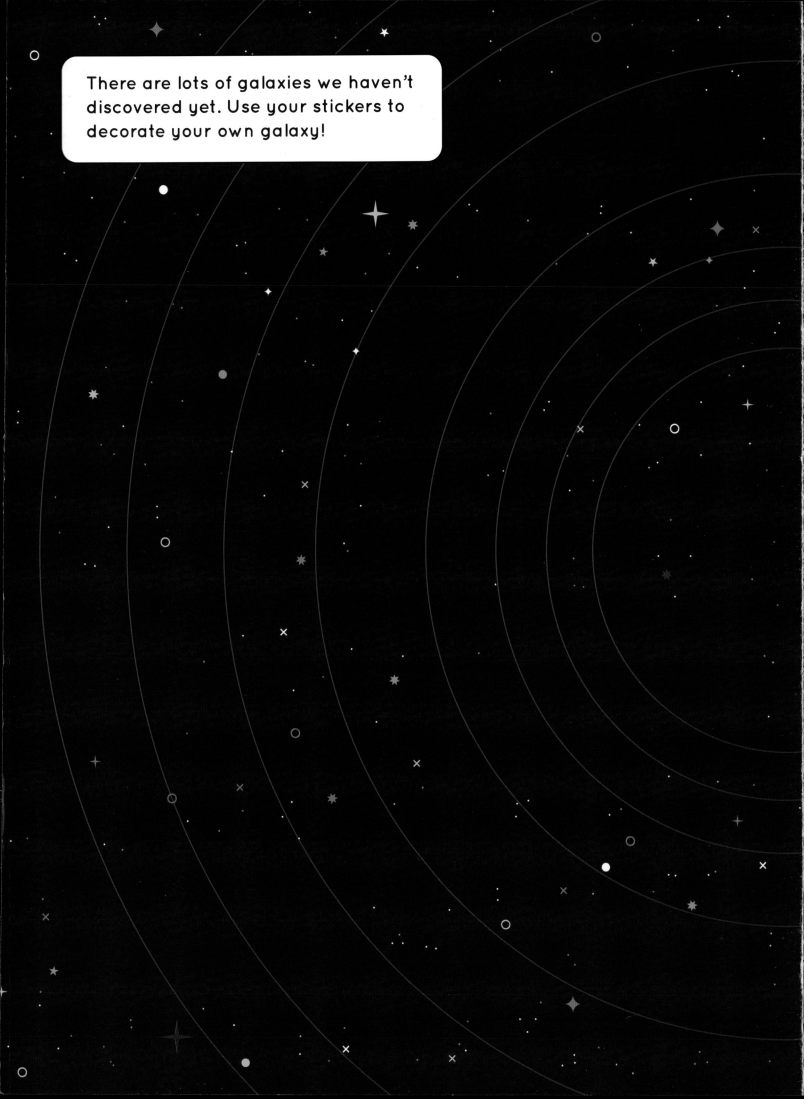

There are lots of galaxies we haven't discovered yet. Use your stickers to decorate your own galaxy!

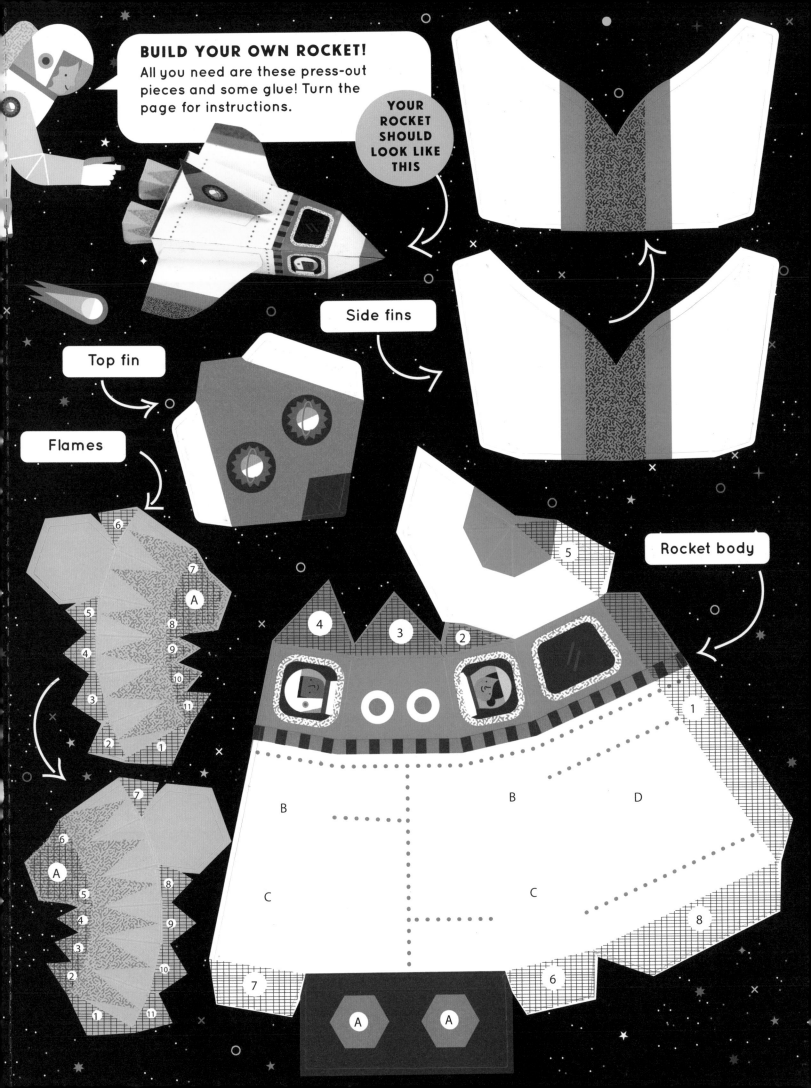

**BUILD YOUR OWN ROCKET!**
All you need are these press-out pieces and some glue! Turn the page for instructions.

YOUR ROCKET SHOULD LOOK LIKE THIS

Side fins

Top fin

Flames

Rocket body

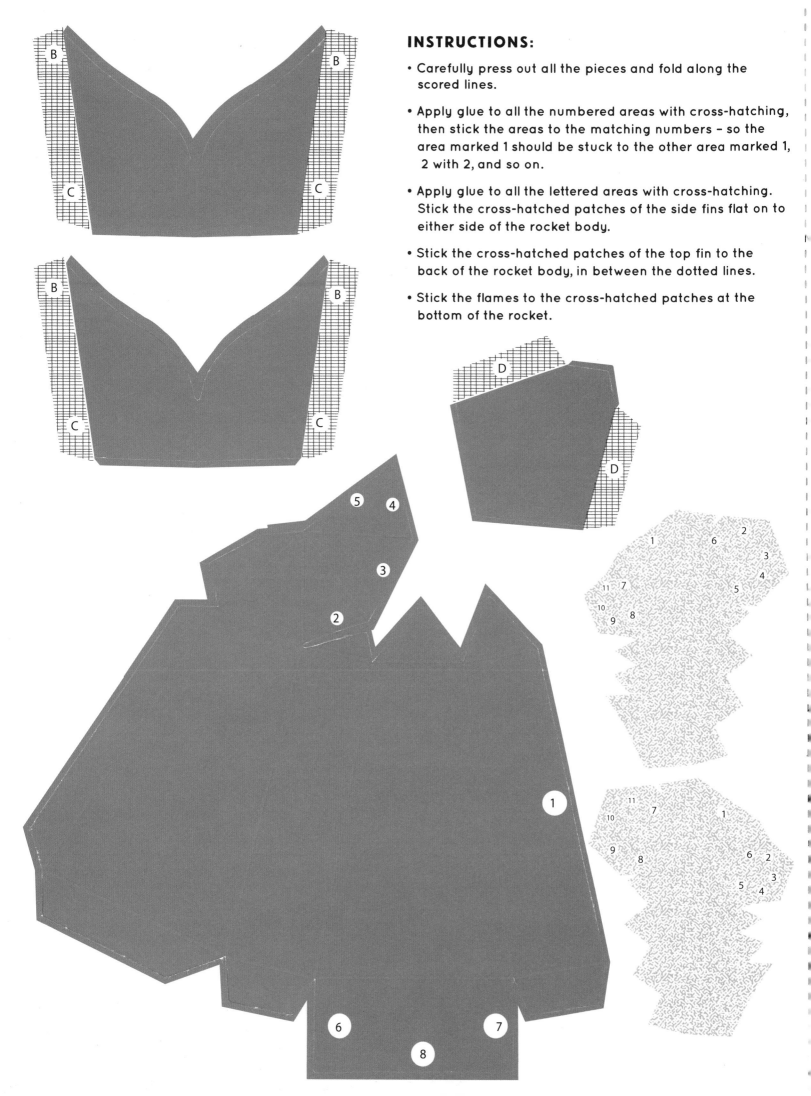

## INSTRUCTIONS:

- Carefully press out all the pieces and fold along the scored lines.

- Apply glue to all the numbered areas with cross-hatching, then stick the areas to the matching numbers – so the area marked 1 should be stuck to the other area marked 1, 2 with 2, and so on.

- Apply glue to all the lettered areas with cross-hatching. Stick the cross-hatched patches of the side fins flat on to either side of the rocket body.

- Stick the cross-hatched patches of the top fin to the back of the rocket body, in between the dotted lines.

- Stick the flames to the cross-hatched patches at the bottom of the rocket.